CW00726426

Creative EMBROIDERY

PRACTICALITIES

Today, creative stitchery is enjoying a worldwide revival. We are very fortunate to have access to an enormous variety of fabrics and threads in hundreds of colours.

Embellishing fabric with stitching has been known since before Roman times and has been not only a popular pastime but also a way of creating something unique to the maker.

We hope you enjoy the delightful designs for home and family in this book.

CHOOSING FABRIC

It is possible to embroider on just about any kind of fabric, natural or man-made, open weave or close, light or dark. Which fabric you choose will determine how your work will look.

Lightweight cottons and linens are ideal for delicate work such as shadow stitch embroidery. DMC's Belfast Art. 3609 or Dublin Art. 3604 were used for projects on page 56.

Heavier weight fabrics are best for the 'more casual' quicker stitches such as long and short stitch and cross stitch. These fabrics are often called, simply, hardanger fabric, DMC Art. 1008 and were used for the cushion on page 48. Choose from a large range of these fabrics in the Zweigart range from DMC.

Use canvas in its various weights from as little as 6 threads to the inch to as many as 22 for petit point, cross stitch and even rug-making from the extensive Zweigart range of fabrics from DMC.

Embroider towels with an even-weave panel for cross stitch called Fingertips, from Charles Craft, distributed by DMC.

CHOOSING THREAD

Embroidery threads come in measured skeins of about 8 m long. Take care when pulling the end out of a new skein that you do not tangle it. Experiment to find the length of working thread that best suits you – generally this will be about 40 cm. Cut your skein into working lengths before you begin stitching and then store them carefully, ready for use. Use either cotton or wool for embroidery, wool being most com-

CONTENTS

monly reserved for canvas work. The following product names and numbers will help you choose the appropriate DMC threads for your embroidery.

DMC Stranded cotton Art. 117 (known as floss) is a glossy, twisted 6 strand thread which is usually separated into 2 or 3 strands for finer work.

Cotton à broder DMC Art. 107 is a single-stranded cotton, similar to pearl cotton but is finer and less shiny. It is easier for children and beginners to use.

Pearl cotton, DMC Art.116/8, 115/3, 115/5 is a shiny 2 ply thread in three weights and is not separated.

Soft embroidery cotton DMC Art. 89 has no shine and being quite thick is mostly used on heavier fabrics.

Stranded pure silk is a very shiny, 7 stranded thread which comes in wonderful colours, ideal for special effects.

Crewel wool or Medici DMC Art. 475 is used for delicate canvas work.

Persian wool is a 3 strand wool which can be divided.

Tapestry wool, DMC Art 486, is a tightly-twisted 4 ply wool, also known as Gobelin wool, and is used for embroidery and canvas work.

CHOOSING NEEDLES

There are three basic types used in needlework – crewel, chenille and tapestry. All three come in a number of sizes and thicknesses. The one you choose depends on the work you are doing, the fabric and the yarn.

Crewels are the sharp-pointed needles most commonly used in embroidery.

Chenilles are thicker and longer than crewels and are best for thicker fabric and yarns.

Tapestry needles have a blunt tip making them most suitable for canvas, tapestry and counted thread work.

HOOPS AND FRAMES

An embroidery hoop or frame is a most useful tool. It helps to keep your work even without too much distortion of the fabric. Hoops keep the fabric taut between two rings and are adjustable to deal with different weights of fabric. If you are working on part of quite a large piece, the hoop will hold that part of it stretched. Frames keep the whole of the work stretched at the same time. You can make your own frame to the size of your work, simply by joining four pieces of wood to form an open square of the right size and tacking your fabric over the frame. The wood, pre-cut and ready to use is available at craft shops.

Craft Editor: Tonia Todman
Managing Editor: Judy Poulos
Editorial Coordinator: Margaret Kelly
Craft Assistants: Martina Oprey; Rosa Alonso; Tina Murphy; Yvonne Deacon; Jocelyn Mitchell; Paula McPhaill
Production Manager: Nadia Sbisa
Layout: Lulu Dougherty
Finished Art: Stephen Joseph
Cover Design: Christie & Eckermann
Illustrations:Lesley Griffith
Photography: Andrew Elton
Publisher: Philippa Sandall

ISBN 1 86343 022 9

Published by J.B. Fairfax Press Pty Ltd
80-82 McLachlan Avenue
Rushcutters Bay 2011
Formatted by J.B. Fairfax Press Pty Ltd
Output by Adtype, Sydney
Printed by Toppan Printing Co, Hong Kong

DISTRIBUTION AND SALES
Newsagent and supermarket distribution
Newsagents Direct Distributors and Storewide Magazine Distributors
150 Bourke Road, Alexandria NSW 2015
Ph: (02) 693 4141 Fax: (02) 669 2305

Sales Enquiries: J.B. Fairfax Press Pty Ltd
Ph: (02) 361 6366 Fax (02) 360 6262

Above: An embroidered jewellery cushion (see page 57)
Left: Three embroidered collars (see pages 26-27)
Right: Embroidering the chintz cushion (see page 43)

STITCH GUIDE

BLANKET STITCH

This stitch is very useful for decorative edging. Working from left to right, bring the needle up at the lower edge and take a stitch from the upper edge back to the lower edge as shown in Fig. 1. Continue to take evenly spaced stitches in this way, keeping the thread under the needle (Fig. 2).

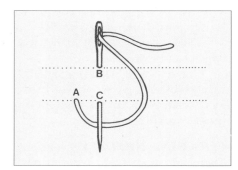

Fig. 1

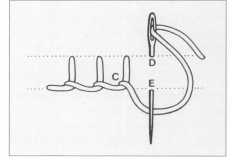

Fig. 2

BULLION STITCH ROSES

Also known as grub roses, these pretty motifs are made from an arrangement of Bullion stitches, worked in toning shades of thread from the darkest in the centre to the lightest at the edge. To make a Bullion stitch, bring the needle to the right side at A and take a stitch to B, bringing the needle up again at A (Fig. 1). Do not pull it through. The distance from A to B equals the length of the final Bullion stitch. Wind the thread around the needle, covering the length from A to B (Fig. 2). Pull the needle through, easing the twisted thread down onto the fabric. Reinsert the needle at B (Fig. 3).

To form the rose, lay down the Bullion stitches, beginning at the centre and building them up in concentric circles with each one at a slight angle to the one before.

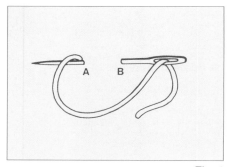

Fig. 1

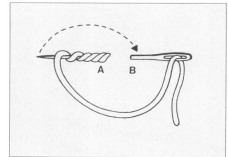

Fig. 2

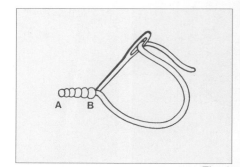

Fig. 3

RAISED BUTTONHOLE STITCH

Buttonhole stitch is worked like Blanket stitch but with the stitches very close together. Outlining the area in small running stitches will give a raised appearance (Fig. 1 and Fig. 2).

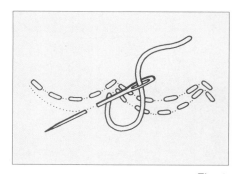

Fig. 1

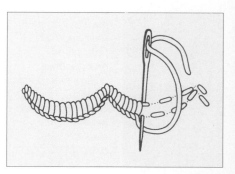

Fig. 2

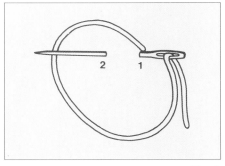

Fig. 1

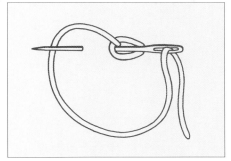

Fig. 2

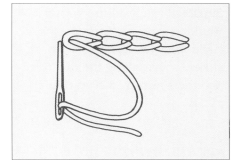

Fig. 3

CHAIN STITCH

Chain stitch is a very versatile embroidery stitch. It can be used in single rows to work a line, to outline or, with rows worked closely together, it can even fill in an area with a block of colour. Work Chain stitch as shown in Fig. 1 and Fig. 2. When the row is complete take a small stitch over the last loop of the chain to secure it as shown in Fig. 3.

CLOSE HERRINGBONE STITCH

This stitch is often used in shadow work embroidery. Working on the wrong side of the work, take a stitch at the lower left outline then take a stitch at the upper outline, bringing the needle out on the wrong side and to the left of the thread. Take a stitch back to the lower outline, bringing the needle out on the wrong side as shown in Fig. 1. Continue to work in this way, crisscrossing from left to right filling in the space required.

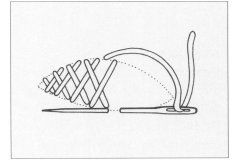

Fig. 1

CROSS STITCH

Cross stitch is the most popular embroidery stitch for almost any type of fabric, especially even-weave fabrics whose threads help you place the stitches. Cross stitch is usually worked in rows of evenly spaced stitches, where one arm of the cross is worked all across the row with the stitches all slanting in the same direction (Fig. 1), then the other arm is worked coming back the other way (Fig. 2). When you work individual Cross stitches make sure that the top arms all run in the same direction.

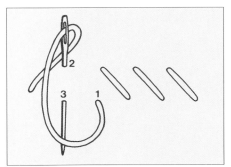

Fig. 1

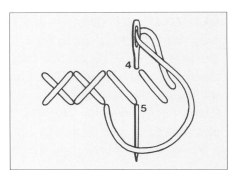

Fig. 2

EYELET STITCH

Outline the area of the eyelet with small running stitches. Make a hole in the centre with sharp scissors or a hole punch. Push the threads through to the wrong side. Working your way around the circle from left to right, stitch closely, overcasting the raw edge and the running stitches (Fig. 2).

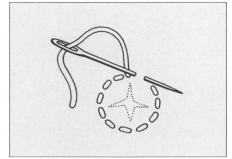

Fig. 1

Fig. 2

FRENCH KNOTS

French Knots are ideal for flower centres. Begin the stitch by bringing the needle up through the fabric and winding the thread around it twice as shown in Fig. 1. Gently pulling the thread tight (Fig. 2), reinsert the needle near the point of exit and pull it through.

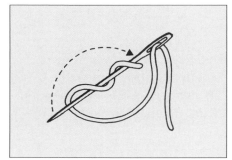
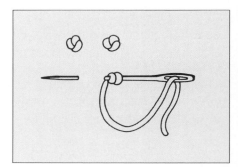

Fig. 1

Fig. 2

HEM STITCH

Draw out the required number of threads from the fabric. Working on the wrong side make small Backstitches to secure thread and then pass the needle from right to left under the required number of threads. (See Fig. 1). Take a small vertical stitch to the right of the thread bundle into the fabric. (See Fig. 2).

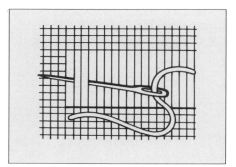
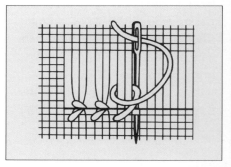

Fig. 1

Fig. 2

LAZY DAISY STITCH

Lazy daisy stitch is popular for working flowers. It is like the last chain of a row of Chain stitch. One stitch gives the impression of a flower petal and groups are usually worked in a circle to look like a flower, as the name implies (see Fig. 1, Fig. 2).

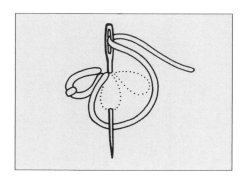
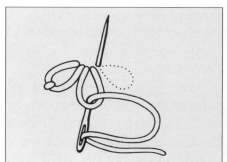

Fig. 1

Fig. 2

LONG AND SHORT STITCH

This stitch (Fig. 1) is often used to fill in areas of colour with a slightly more textured effect than Satin stitch. You can shade colours with this stitch by stitching one set of Long and Short stitches in one colour and the next set in a slightly lighter or darker shade, blending them in quite smoothly.

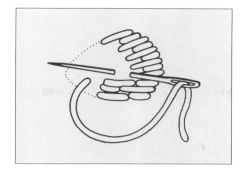

Fig. 1

OVERCAST STITCH

Use running stitch to outline the design then work Overcast stitches as shown in Fig. 1, very close together, covering the running stitches.

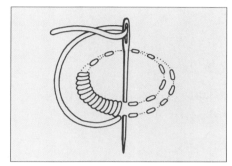

Fig. 1

RAISED SATIN STITCH

This stitch is used to give a slightly padded look to embroidery. Using small running stitches, outline and fill in the area to be covered (Fig. 1). Beginning just outside the outlining stitches and working from left to right for horizontal stitches (top to bottom for vertical stitches), work stitches close together as shown in Fig. 2.

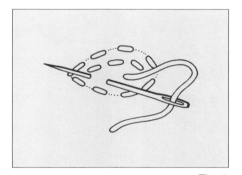

Fig. 1

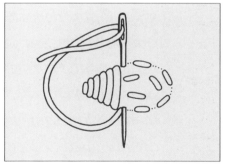

Fig. 2

STEM STITCH

This is mainly an outlining stitch which as its name implies is often used to work the stems on floral motifs. Simply work a Long stitch then come up again half a stitch back as in Fig. 1, keeping the thread below the needle. Repeat as shown in Fig. 2.

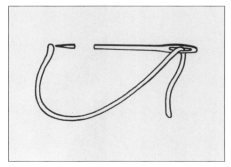

Fig. 1

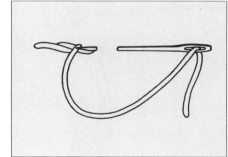

Fig. 2

Perfect
White Plus

The colour of innocence and purity: white is the perfect choice for elegant linen and exquisite underwear. The delightful floral motif we have chosen makes this charming embroidered tablecloth and matching napkins very special. Sheer cotton organdie is perfect for the delicate shadow work while the clear outlines of neatly mitred corners add a classic edge to this heirloom for tomorrow. The same techniques are also used to decorate the delicate camisole and pants.

TABLECLOTH AND NAPKINS

Naturally, you can choose any size you wish for your tablecloth, but in practical terms the size will be limited by the width of the fabric. If you must join lengths of fabric to achieve the width you desire, then take care to place the seams at the table edge and not down the centre of the cloth.

MATERIALS

a square of cotton organdie, the size of your choice
45 cm squares of organdie for each napkin
sewing thread
stranded embroidery threads in the following DMC colours:
986 (dark green) and white
a suitable needle

METHOD

See the Pull Out Transfer Sheet at the back of the book for the floral motif transfer.
The same basic method is used to make the tablecloth and the napkins.

1 *To prepare your square:* Straighten all the edges of your square of organdie and cut away the selvages. Make sure that the edges follow the grain of the fabric and are not on the bias. Press in 1 cm hems all around the edges. Press in the true hemline 4 cm away from the pressed edge.

2 *To mitre the corner:* Fold the corner to the wrong side as shown in Fig. 1, making sure the pressed lines are aligned. Press. Repeat this for each corner. Open out the corners and fold the whole square of fabric in half diagonally, with right sides together and pressed edges

even. Stitch along the pressed line as shown in Fig. 2. Trim the fabric at the point and press the seam open as shown in Fig. 3. Turn the corner to the right side. Repeat this for all four corners. Press the corners and hems carefully. Stitch hems into place.

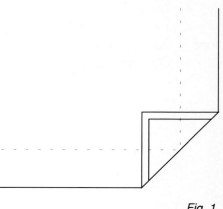

Fig. 1

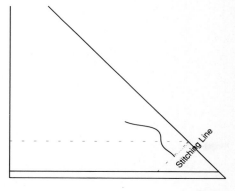

Fig. 2

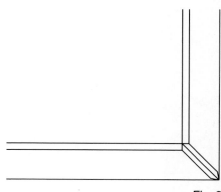

Fig. 3

STITCHES USED
Close Herringbone stitch for the shadow work leaves; Satin stitch for the flowers; Stem stitch for the stems

3 *For the embroidery:* Locate the transfer for the floral motif on the Transfer Sheet. Press the transfer designs into place on the tablecloth, following the directions on the Transfer Sheet. Embroider the leaves, stems and flowers in shadow work, using two strands of embroidery thread and following our Stitch Guide and illustrations at the front of the book. Press the tablecloth and napkins carefully.

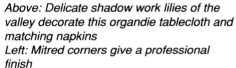

Above: Delicate shadow work lilies of the valley decorate this organdie tablecloth and matching napkins
Left: Mitred corners give a professional finish

11

CAMISOLE AND PANTS

Delicate underwear is the perfect foil for shadow work embroidery but keep it simple. These bows are the perfect choice.

Note that the camisole and pants are bias-cut.

MATERIALS

1.6 m of 115 cm wide cotton voile
4.5 m of double-edged lace for
   trimming
tracing paper
pencil
sewing thread
stranded embroidery thread in DMC
   798 (mid-blue) or the colour
   of your choice
embroidery needle
elastic

METHOD

See the Pull Out Pattern Sheet at the back of the book for the pattern.
See the Pull Out Transfer Sheet at the back of the book for the embroidery motif.
Pattern Outline ————
1 cm seams allowed all around each pattern piece.

1 *For cutting out:* Trace the pattern pieces from the pattern sheet. Cut out the pattern pieces from your fabric as directed on the Pattern Sheet, noting that they are cut on the bias of the fabric.

2 *For the embroidery:* Press the transfer designs into place on the Camisole and Pants following the directions on the Transfer Sheet. Embroider the bows in shadow work, following the directions for Close Herringbone stitch and Overcast stitch in the Stitch Guide at the front of the book. Take care not to distort the fabric while you are embroidering – a frame will help you with this.

3 *For the sewing:* Make all seams French seams or normal seams, trimming the seam allowances to 6 mm, then neatening them with zigzag stitching or overlocking. Place the front and back camisole pieces together with raw edges even. Stitch the side seams. Place the front and back pants pieces together at the inside legs with raw edges even. Stitch the inside leg seams. Prepare and stitch the crotch seam in the same way, stitching from the front waist through the crotch to the back waist.

4 *For the elastic:* Turn 6 mm at the waist edge to the wrong side to neaten, then turn again 1.5 cm. Stitch all around to form a casing for the elastic, leaving a gap for inserting elastic. Insert the elastic, try on the pants and adjust the elastic for comfort. Overlap the ends and stitch together. Close the gap in the casing by hand.

5 *For the lace:* Attach lace to the camisole's upper and lower edges, and the leg edges of the pants in the following way. Position the lace so that approximately $7/8$ of the lace sits on the fabric and $1/8$ is over the edge. Where necessary fold the lace into mitres or angles that will allow it to follow the fabric shape. Set your sewing machine stitch controls to a narrow zigzag stitch that is almost a Satin stitch. Stitch around the pattern of the lace close to the inner edge. Trim away the voile from underneath the lace and the excess lace inside the stitching on the right side. Oversew any angles or mitres that need to be secured, using a narrow zigzag stitch.

STITCHES USED
Close Herringbone stitch for the shadow work bows

Top left: The shadow work bow seen from the right side
Above left: The same bow viewed from the wrong side
Above: The camisole and pants with lace trim and embroidered bows

6 *For the straps:* Measure the length for your shoulder straps and cut two pieces of bias fabric this length plus 3 cm x 2 cm. Fold the straps over double with right sides together and long edges matching. Stitch twice for strength along the long side. Turn the straps to the right side. Pin the straps in place on the front and back of the camisole so that the raw ends of the straps are tucked underneath, out of sight. Try on the camisole to adjust the strap length then handsew the ends into place.

To turn rouleau straps if you don't own a gadget made specially for the purpose, thread a large darning needle with a strong, double thread. Stitch securely at one end of the rouleau, then pass the needle down the length and out the other end. Pulling gently on the double thread, turn the rouleau to the right side.

Trousseau Treasures

*Not so long ago, young girls
began preparing and putting
aside beautiful bed linen and towels
for a 'hope chest' or 'glory box'.
These days, although the pace of life
seems to have overtaken
this charming old tradition,
hand-embroidered treasures like
these still delight the bride-to-be.*

*Clockwise from the left: The voile nightgown; cushion, p. 46;
embroidered sheets and pillowcases; Bullion stitch rose
embroidered towels and cross stitch embroidered towels*

A VOILE NIGHTGOWN

A soft, pure cotton, voile nightgown that's been embroidered with loving care would be a delightful addition to any trousseau. This simple style has been trimmed with lace and shadow work bows, and scattered with Bullion stitch roses.

MATERIALS

2.7 m of 115 cm wide cotton voile

2.5 m of good quality bias binding (either cotton or satin)

2.5 m of very fine piping cord

2.5 m of 1 cm wide white satin ribbon for facing

2 m of ribbon in the same colour as the shadow work embroidery for the bow

4 m of 7 cm wide lace for the bodice and hem trim

stranded embroidery threads in the colours of your choice or DMC colours 793 (dark blue), 794 (light blue), 988 (green) and white matching sewing thread

a suitable embroidery needle

METHOD

See the Pull Out Transfer Sheet at the back of the book for the bow motif. See the Pull Out Pattern Sheet at the back of the book for the nightgown pattern.

Pattern Outline ————

1 cm seams allowed all around each pattern piece.

1 *For cutting out:* Cut out the nightgown front and back pattern pieces as directed on the Pattern Sheet. Cut approximately 2 m of 3 cm wide bias strips from the fabric for shoulder straps.

2 *For the embroidery:* Iron the bow motif onto the centre front of the nightgown, following the directions on the Transfer Sheet. Embroider the motif using two strands of embroidery thread in Close Herringbone stitch, French Knots and the Bullion stitch roses as instructed in the Stitch Guide

at the front of the book. Embroider the roses around the bow.

3 *For the lace and piping:* Gather the lace just enough to cause it to stand away from the fabric when applied. Press open the bias binding and then fold it over double, with wrong sides together. Using the zipper foot of your sewing machine, stitch the piping cord into the fold of the bias binding.

4 *For the sewing:* Join the front to the back nightgown at the side seams using narrow French seams or a normal seam with the allowance stitched together 6 mm from the seam, trimmed back close to the stitching and overcast. Be sure to leave one side seam open for up to 30 cm from hem for a split.

5 *For the lace:* With the wrong side of the lace facing the right side of the nightgown and raw edges matching, baste the lace around the hem and around the side split. Make small pleats if necessary to ease the lace around the corners and curves. Gradually ease the lace away to nothing at the top of the split so that it looks as if it disappears into the top of the split. Using a fine zigzag stitch and sewing 6 mm in from the edge, stitch the lace around the hem and side split. Trim away the seam allowances close to the stitching. Starting at a side seam, baste the lace around the upper bodice in the same way as for the hem.

6 *For the piping:* Pin and baste the piping on top of the lace at the upper bodice, with raw edges match-

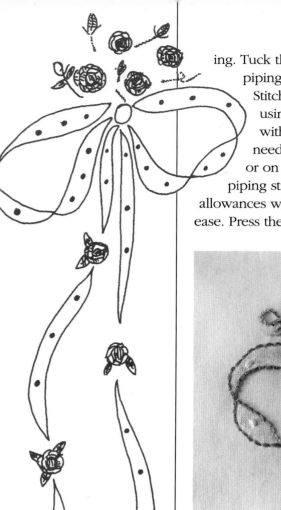

ing. Tuck the raw end of the piping under at the overlap. Stitch the piping in place using the zipper foot and with the sewing machine needle nearer to the cord or on top of the previous piping stitching. Clip the seam allowances where necessary for ease. Press the seam to the inside.

Above: The top of the nightgown showing the delicate lace, piping and rouleau shoulder straps
Left: A shadow work embroidered bow and Bullion stitch roses trim the lovely nightgown

7 *For the shoulder straps:* Fold the bias strips of fabric in half lengthways with right sides together and raw edges even. Stitch down the long side, trim the seam and turn the straps to the right side. Try on the nightgown to adjust the length of the shoulder straps. Using two lengths of rouleau for each shoulder, fold each length in half and loop one through the other in the middle, so that the loop sits on the shoulder and the raw ends are at the front and the back. Handsew the raw ends in place. On the inside, handsew the 1 cm wide ribbon over the seam allowance with the top edge of the ribbon on the piping stitching, pleating the ribbon where necessary around

the angles and covering the ends of the shoulder straps. Make two thread loops on the side seams at waist level, or just above, to hold the ribbon.

To turn rouleau straps if you don't own a gadget made specially for the purpose, thread a large darning needle with a strong, double thread. Stitch securely at one end of the rouleau, then pass the needle down through the length and out the other end. Pulling gently on the double thread, turn the rouleau to the right side.

EMBROIDERED TOWELS

You can buy towels with the even-weave fabric panel already included and ready to be embroidered. If you can't buy them where you shop, you can find an even-weave band (known as Aida) at craft shops, for you to embroider then sew onto the towel when you've completed your stitching. Either way, these charming confections of ribbons, roses, rabbits and hearts should grace any bathroom.

MATERIALS
a suitable towel with or without an
even-weave band
an even-weave band to embroider
stranded embroidery threads in colours
of your choice. We used DMC
colours 3354, 800 and white
a suitable embroidery needle

METHOD
See the Pull Out Pattern Sheet at the back of the book for the embroidery graphs.

1 *For the Cross stitch towel:* Find the centre of the band to be embroidered by folding or measuring. Sew lines of loose running stitch along the folds. The intersection of these lines marks the centre point which corresponds with the centre of the design. To find the centre of the design, join the arrows at each side with a ruler. The point where they intersect is the centre.

2 Each square on the design graph represents one cross stitch and the symbol indicates the colour to be used in the embroidery. Cross stitch the motifs following the Stitch Guide at the

front of the book, counting the threads and using the design graph as a guide for your stitches. Do not pull the threads too tightly and make sure you begin and end by running the needle through the back of a few stitches to secure the ends.

3 If you are using an even-weave band, turn under the raw ends and machine stitch the band in place across the towel.

For the Bullion stitch rose towels: Stitch sprays of Bullion stitch roses, following the Stitch Guide at the front of the book. Trim with bands of lace and ribbon or satin ribbon-trimmed grosgrain as shown. Tie the ribbon into a bow and secure with small stitches.

There is no prettier way to dress up your bathroom than with a pile of fluffy, embroidered bath towels, face cloths and matching hand towels.

STITCHES USED
Cross stitch for the rabbits and hearts; Bullion stitch roses and leaves

EMBROIDERED BED LINEN

There is nothing like the feeling of slipping between crisp cotton sheets. These ones have an heirloom quality in their pretty embroidery. Trim the bed linen with colours that accent your bedroom scheme and add some beautiful cotton lace for that final touch.

MATERIALS

purchased cotton pillowcases and one flat cotton sheet
stranded embroidery threads in colours of your choice. We used DMC colours 783, 445, 307 and 444
12 cm wide cotton, single-edged lace
12 mm wide satin ribbon
a suitable embroidery needle

METHOD

See the Pull Out Transfer Sheet at the back of the book for the embroidery designs.

PILLOWCASE

1 *For the ribbon and lace:* Pin the lace around the pillowcase opening, so that the lacy edge just overhangs the pillowcase opening, beginning and ending at a side seam. Take care not to catch the pillow shield. Open the pillowcase stitching at that point for 12 cm to allow the raw ends of the lace to be pushed through to the wrong side. Stitch the lace in place. Pin and stitch the ribbon in place so that it covers the raw edge of the lace, pushing its ends through the gap as well. Stitch the gap closed.

2 *For the design:* Find and mark the centre of the lace on top of the pillowcase by measuring or folding it in half. Locate the monogram and floral design on the Transfer Sheet and iron the transfers onto the centre of the lace as instructed on the Transfer Sheet.

3 *For the embroidery:* Embroider the motifs using two strands of thread and following the Stitch Guide at the front of the book. Press.

SHEETS

Follow steps 1, 2 and 3 in the Method, omitting the instructions relating to the opening of the side seams of the pillowcase.

STITCHES USED

Raised Satin stitch for the monograms, flowers and leaves; Eyelet stitch for flower centres; Stem stitch for the stems

THE ROSE GARDEN

Bullion stitch roses are a charming embroidery motif for delicate lingerie, bath towels, sleep wear or bed linen. The arrangement of the roses need only be limited by your imagination. Here are a few ideas to inspire you. Note that you can combine Bullion stitch roses with many other embroidery stitches, such as the French Knots indicated here by circles, to give the effect you are looking for. On the next page you will see how designs like these have been applied in actual embroidery.

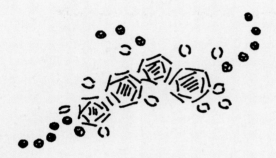

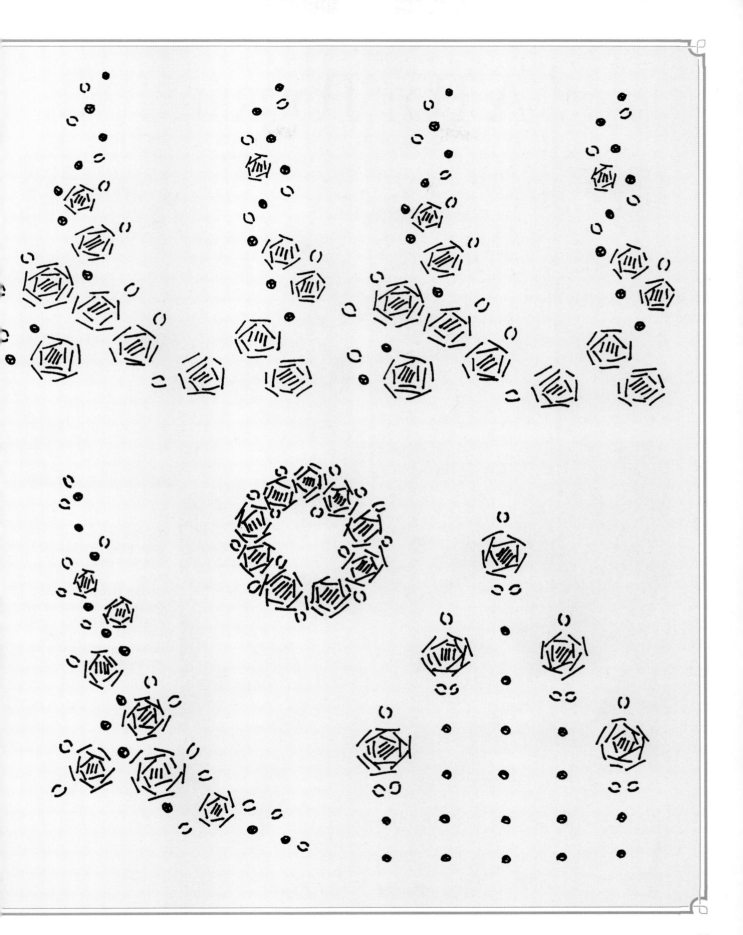

A POT POURRI

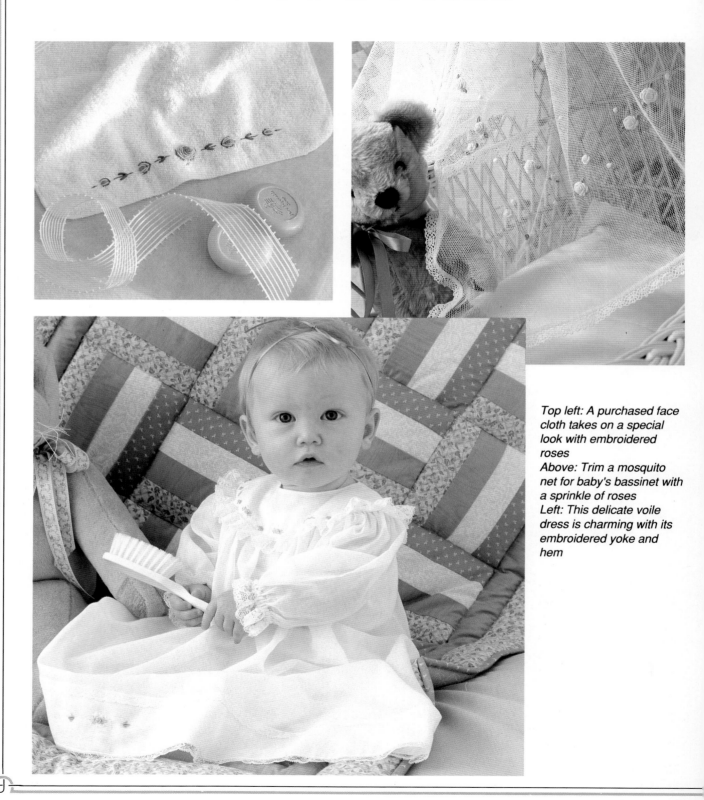

Top left: A purchased face cloth takes on a special look with embroidered roses

Above: Trim a mosquito net for baby's bassinet with a sprinkle of roses

Left: This delicate voile dress is charming with its embroidered yoke and hem

Right: Pretty as well as practical, this bathrobe is a touch of luxury
Below right: For the bride and groom on their wedding day, embroider a cover for their wedding photo album
Below: Dainty Bullion stitch roses are the perfect finishing touch for these lingerie bags

A Collar Story

A crisp, white collar can add the finishing touch to any young lady's special outfit. Even better if the collar is embroidered or personally monogrammed with her initials. Make the collar removable for washing, then she won't have to keep it for 'best' but can wear it anytime at all.

ORGANDIE COLLAR

Scallops of traditional organdie, delicately embroidered, make this collar ideal for a seven-year-old girl.

MATERIALS

50 cm of 90 cm wide cotton organdie
tracing paper
pencil
stranded embroidery threads in your
  choice of colours
matching sewing thread
a suitable embroidery needle

METHOD

See the Pull Out Pattern Sheet at the back of the book for the collar pattern. See the Pull Out Transfer Sheet at the back of the book for the embroidery designs.

Pattern Outline ——————

1 cm seams allowed all around each pattern piece.

1 *For cutting out:* Trace the complete collar pattern from the Pattern Sheet, using the tracing paper and pencil. Transfer any symbols and markings. Using this as your pattern, cut out two fronts and four backs from organdie (one front and two backs will be the facing). Trace the scalloped border pattern from the complete collar pattern on the Pattern Sheet. Using this as your guide, cut out a scalloped border strip for each front and both backs (two front borders and four back borders in total). Cut a strip of fabric 38 cm x 6 cm for the neckband.

2 *For the sewing:* Pin the extra scalloped border strips to the outer edges of each collar piece. Baste all around and from here on treat these as a single piece. Join the collar front to the collar backs at the shoulders. Repeat this for the facing. Place the collar and facing together, so that raw edges are even. Stitch around all the edges. Trim the fabric at the corners and clip the seams where necessary for ease. Turn the collar to the right side, pushing out the fabric very carefully around the scalloped edges. Baste the neckband around the collar neckline, with right sides facing and raw edges even. Stitch around the neckline. Fold the neckband in to the wrong side and press under 6 mm on remaining raw edge of neckband. Fold neckband in half lengthways with right sides facing. Stitch across the short ends 1.5 cm beyond the edges of the scallops. Turn the collar to the right side, and handsew the inner folded edge to the neckline stitching. Stitch carefully along the inner edge of the border through all thicknesses, joining the collar and the facing. Make a buttonhole on the right back band at the neck edge. Sew on the button to correspond with the buttonhole.

3 *For the embroidery:* Embroider the Bullion stitch roses as shown, following the Stitch Guide at the front of the book.

STITCHES USED

Bullion stitch for the roses and leaves; Stem stitch for the stems

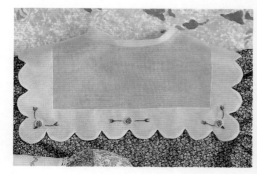

CIRCULAR LINEN COLLAR

MATERIALS

35 cm of 90 cm wide handkerchief-
    weight linen
tracing paper
pencil
stranded embroidery threads in the
    colours of your choice. We have used
    DMC colours 368; 3347; 603; 605;
    796; 800; 3078; 761; 211; 818
1.5 m narrow cotton lace
one small flat button
matching sewing thread
a suitable embroidery needle

METHOD

See the Pull Out Transfer Sheet at the
back of the book for the collar shape
and embroidery designs.
1 cm seams allowed all around each
pattern piece.

1 *For cutting out:* Cut out the
pattern piece from the Transfer
Sheet and iron the entire transfer onto
a single layer of fabric. Cut out the
collar shape. Note that the cutting line
is the transfer line at the edge of the
collar and that 1 cm seam allowances
have been included. Using the transfer
paper as your pattern, cut out another
collar shape. Cut two 35 cm x 3 cm
bias strips of linen for the neckline
bands which extend into the ties.

2 *For the embroidery:* Embroider the
flowers on the collar front using
two strands of embroidery thread,
following the Stitch Guide in the front
of the book.

3 *For the neckbands:* Fold the strip
of fabric for the neckbands over
double lengthways with right sides

together. Stitch across both short ends
and down the raw long edge of each
neckband, leaving a 17 cm gap in the
stitching at one end. Turn the ties to
the right side and press carefully. Baste
the 17 cm raw edges of the ties to the
neckline of the embroidered collar,
starting 1 cm from the back opening,
and so that the neckbands meet at the
centre front.

4 *To finish off:* Stitch the lace around
the embroidered collar, so that the
straight edge of the lace lies 1 cm from
the edge of the collar and the lace
points towards the neck edge. Pin and
baste the remaining plain collar piece
over the embroidered collar. Stitch
around all the edges, following the
stitching line for the lace and the
neckbands, and leaving an opening in
one centre back edge for turning. Trim
the corners and clip into the curved
seams for ease. Turn the collar to the
right side, handsew the opening closed
and press it carefully. Make a buttonhole on the right centre back at the
neck edge. Sew a button on the left
side to correspond with the buttonhole. Make a bow with the ties at the
centre front.

*Fine linen is the
perfect choice for a
delicate collar,
monogrammed and
embroidered, for a
five-year-old little
miss.*

STITCHES USED

Raised Satin stitch for the
flowers, leaves and bow
centres; Eyelet stitch for
the flower centres; Stem
stitch for the stems and
outline; Long and Short
stitch for the bows

TIE-ON BABY'S COLLAR

This sweet tie-on collar for babies will stay in place no matter how much they wriggle or how many cuddles they get.

STITCHES USED

Raised Satin stitch for the monogram, flowers and leaves; Eyelet stitch for the flowers centres; Stem stitch for the stems and outlining; Long and Short stitch for the bows; Blanket stitch for the edging

MATERIALS

40 cm of 90 cm wide handkerchief-weight linen
80 cm of 1 cm wide satin ribbon for side ties (or you can make linen ties from scraps)
3 small, flat buttons
stranded embroidery thread in colours of your choice. We have used DMC colours 827; 3716; 962; 772; 211; 746; 445; 471
sewing thread
a suitable embroidery needle

METHOD

See the Pull Out Pattern Sheet at the back of the book for the collar pattern. See the Pull Out Transfer Sheet at the back of the book for the embroidery motifs.

Pattern Outline ————
1 cm seams allowed all around each pattern piece.

1 *For cutting out:* Cut out the front and back collar pattern pieces as directed on the Pattern Sheet. Be sure to cut two fronts, four backs and four collar pieces.

2 *For the embroidery:* Locate the monogram you require and the floral motif on the Transfer Sheet. Iron the motifs onto one front collar piece. Embroider the motifs in two strands of embroidery thread following the Stitch Guide at the front of the book. You may like to embroider the motifs using threads in shades that reflect the colours of the dress over which the collar is worn, or you may like to make it quite neutral so that it can be worn with several dresses.

3 *For the sewing:* When you have finished the embroidery, press the fabric pieces carefully, then join the front to the backs at the shoulders. Place the small curved collar pieces together in pairs, with right sides together and raw edges even. Stitch around the curved edges. Clip into the curves for ease. Turn the small collars to the right side. Press.

4 *To assemble the collars:* Stitch around each small collar and the main collar with small buttonhole stitches in a colour used in the flower embroidery, using two strands of thread. Baste the small collars around the neckline of the main embroidered collar pieces. Pin one 20 cm length of ribbon 2 cm above each lower outer corner (two on the front and one each on the backs) with raw edges matching. Place main collars together with right sides facing. Stitch around the edge, leaving an opening for turning along one centre back edge. Take care not to catch the ties as you sew. Trim seams and corners, clipping where necessary for ease. Turn the collar right side out and press. Close the opening by hand.

5 *To finish off:* Make three buttonholes on the right back, placing one at the neckline and the others 6 cm apart. Sew the buttons on the left back to correspond with the buttonholes.

Fit for a Princess

She will certainly look like a princess in her special dress with its traditional smocking and embroidery.

SIMPLE SMOCKING

Smocking began as the first 'elastic' but has become a delightful and creative technique for trimming babies' and children's clothes. Follow these illustrated steps to master the technique and some of the most common smocking stitches.

1 Mark dots on wrong side of fabric with a purchased smocking dot transfer or by tracing them off graph paper with clear points. You can also place carbon paper under the fabric and, pinning graph paper on top, firmly press out dots.

2 Gathering up dots: Using strong, doubled thread in a contrasting colour, begin at right-hand side and pick up each dot across fabric. Leave threads hanging at ends.

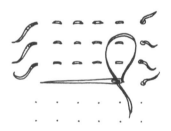

3 Pulling up: Pull up threads to desired width, for example width of yoke. Tie off threads firmly in pairs. Pull up firmly, but not tightly. Secure threads. Begin smocking on right-hand side. Remove gathering threads when smocking is complete.

OUTLINE STITCH: Work stitch with thread above needle as shown and keeping stitches tight.

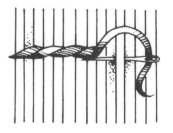

WAVE STITCH: Work stitches firmly although angles make this stitch very elastic. Always work between two rows of gathering stitches, beginning at lower left corner and working up as shown.

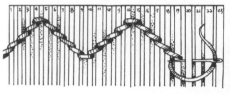

When ascending, thread lies under needle and below when descending.

HONEYCOMBING STITCH: One of the oldest smocking stitches, it is very elastic and simple to do. Stagger starting points of stitches, working over two folds.

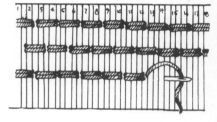

SURFACE HONEYCOMB: This stitch is elastic and very decorative, exposing more thread. It can be built up into panels by mirror reversing the panels.

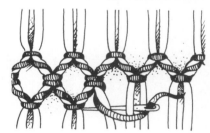

BULLION KNOTS: Are worked as if embroidering, but take care to begin and end stitches on folds as shown.

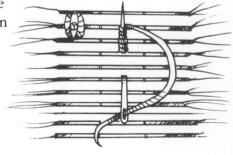

SMOCKED DRESS
FOR A FIVE-YEAR-OLD

DETACHABLE COLLAR

See the Pull Out Transfer Sheet at the back of the book for the smocking dots.

1 Using the dress front as your pattern, trace a piece that follows the neckline and shoulder lines. Mark points 8 cm from the neckline in an arc from one shoulder to the other. Repeat this for the back. These pieces will form the underlay of the smocked collar that tucks inside the dress neck. Cut one front and two backs of this pattern from the dress fabric, taking care to cut them along straight grainlines. Join the front and backs of the underlay pieces at the shoulders. Neaten the outside edge by hemming, overlocking or zigzag stitching.

2 Cut out the collar, using the pattern in the pattern packet, from the dress fabric and not from the lace as shown on the pattern packet. Smock the collar as instructed in the pattern packet and in 'Simple Smocking' on page 34. Press under 1 cm on the outer edge of the smocked collar. Stitch.

3 Ease the collar to the size of the neckline and baste it around the neckline of the underlay. Cut a 4.5 cm wide bias strip from the fabric. Press it over double with right sides together. Place this bias on top of the collar with all raw edges matching. Stitch it in place, joining the underlay, collar and bias strip as you sew.

4 Make a thread loop on the centre right back and sew a small button onto the left centre back to correspond with the loop. You may like to have small press studs on the inside shoulder of the dress and on the collar underlay to help keep the collar in place.

SLEEVES

See the Pull Out Transfer Sheet at the back of the book for the smocking dots.

1 Find the centre of the sleeve pattern by folding it in half and rule a line from the top to the lower edge. Cut through the pattern along this line. Place the pattern pieces onto the fabric, spreading the two halves 15 cm apart. Iron on smocking dots 4 cm deep across the sleeves, 4 cm from the lower edge. Smock the sleeves in the same stitches as were used on the collar.

2 Press under 1 cm on the sleeve ends. Baste lace under this edge as for the collar. Stitch. Stitch the underarm seam. Gather the sleeve cap and sew sleeves into dress armholes. Neaten armhole edges with overlocking or zigzag stitching.

This lovely little dress has two detachable collars – one smocked to match the dress and the other taken from A Collar Story on page 26 embroidered with flowers. We have used Simplicity pattern No. 9579 for the dress. Follow the pattern instructions but take note of our changes to the Collar and Sleeves instructions.

STITCHES USED
Honeycomb stitch and Surface Honeycomb stitch

SMOCKED DRESS
FOR A SEVEN-YEAR OLD

*We have added
smocking and
coloured piping to
this otherwise simple
dress made from
New Look pattern
No. 6232. The
detachable organdie
collar from 'A Collar
Story' is embroidered
to reflect the print in
the dress fabric and
more small Bullion
stitch roses have been
added to the sleeve
cuffs. The smocking
is also in colours to
match the dress.*

Select from any of the smocking
stitches shown on page 34 to smock
the panel in the centre front of the
dress. Follow the pattern maker's
instructions for making the dress, but
note our changes below.

1 *For the smocking on the skirt:*
See the Pull Out Transfer Sheet at
the back of the book for the smocking
dots.
Divide the skirt width into eight
panels. Transfer the smocking dots to
the centre six panels of the skirt,
leaving one panel clear on either side.
Gather up the dots and embroider
smocking to the desired depth, using
the stitches in our 'Simple Smocking'
guide on page 34. Make sure the
finished width of the skirt matches the

lower edge of the bodice. Read the
piping instructions before joining the
skirt to the bodice.

2 *For the piping at waist and cuffs:*
In addition to the materials listed
on the pattern packet you will need a
length of toning bias binding and
piping cord, long enough to go
around the waist and both cuffs.
Open out the length of toning bias
binding. Press, then fold it over double
catching a length of narrow piping
cord in the fold. When you have
assembled the bodice, baste the piping
around the lower edge of the bodice,
with the piping on right side of fabric
and keeping raw edges even. Attach
skirt as instructed. Repeat these steps
around the lower edges of the sleeves
after gathering but
before attaching
the cuffs.

3 *For the
Bullion stitch
roses:* Make small
Bullion stitch roses
using two or three
strands of thread at
the centre of the
cuffs, following the
instructions in the
Stitch Guide at the
front of the book.
Make as many as
you like to form a
pleasing pattern.

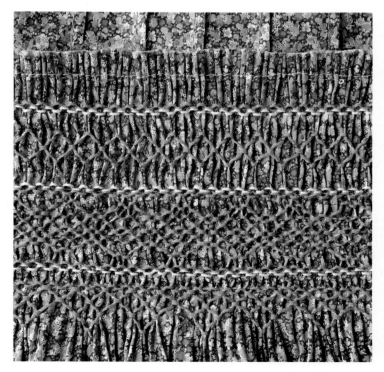

*Left: Close up of the
smocking*

STITCHES USED
Surface Honeycomb stitch

SMOCKED DRESS
FOR A BABY

SIZE: 6 to 12 months

MATERIALS
1.10 m of 115 cm wide fabric
three small buttons
1.2 m cotton lace
embroidery thread for smocking
tracing paper and pencil

METHOD
See the Pull Out Pattern Sheet at the back of the book for the pattern. See the Pull Out Transfer Sheet at the back of the book for the smocking dots.
Pattern Outline ——•• ——
1 cm seams allowed all around each pattern piece.

1 *For cutting out:* Trace the pattern pieces off the Pattern Sheet. Cut out the pattern pieces as instructed.

2 *For the smocking:* Smock the dress front following the instructions in Simple Smocking on page 34. Pull up the smocking to the width of the front yoke.

3 *For the yoke:* Sew front yoke to back yokes at shoulders with right sides facing. Press seams open. Sew the front yoke facing to the back yoke facings (extensions of back yoke), with right sides together. Press seams open. Fold yoke facings over yokes so that right sides are facing. Stitch around the neck edge. Trim the seam, clip curves. Turn the facing to the right side. Press. Pin front yoke to front skirt with right sides facing. Stitch, taking care to leave the front yoke facing free.

4 *For the skirt:* Stitch the centre back skirt seam up to the opening. Neaten the skirt back opening edges. Pin the back yokes to the back skirt as far as the foldline on the back yokes. Fold the back extensions to the inside along the foldlines, forming facings. Stitch through all thicknesses, taking care to leave the back yoke facing free. Press all seams towards yoke. Turn under seam allowance on raw lower edges of yokes.

5 *For the sleeves:* Baste together the raw armhole edges of the yokes and from here on treat them as a single layer. Gather the sleeve heads. Sew the sleeves into the armholes, adjusting the gathering to fit. Neaten the armhole edges with overlocking or zigzag stitching. Turn under 4 cm at the sleeve ends. Stitch the raw edge down with two rows of stitching to form the casings. Join the ends of the lace and stitch it around the sleeve ends, just under the edge as shown. Thread elastic through the casings, adjust the length and secure the ends.

6 *To finish off:* Sew the side seams from wrist to hem. Turn up the skirt hem. Press. Join the ends of the lace together. Baste the lace around the hem, just under the edge as shown. Stitch, fixing the hem and lace in place as you go. Make buttonholes in back yoke. Sew on buttons.

STITCHES USED
Honeycomb stitch; Surface Honeycomb stitch; Outline stitch; Wave stitch; Bullion stitch

THE SMOCKING STORY

Smocking is a technique of decorating fabric which actually becomes part of the shaping and construction of the garment. As a technique it has been around for hundreds of years and probably long before that. Because of the perishable nature of cotton fabric, there are few examples of very old smocking but we have evidence from the paintings of the fifteenth century that smocked garments were in vogue even then. Originally, clothing was simply cut and with little or no shaping, apart from being caught up in a belt or a girdle. Later, as a more generous use of fabric became the practice, a way had to be found to drape and shape fabric to the body and then to secure that shaping in some way, and smocking was born. Not only did smocking shape the garment but it added some elasticity and a way of adding decoration at the same time.

The earliest reference using the word 'smocking' dates from the fourteenth century. The technique seems to take its name from the smocks which were worn by the wealthy as an undergarment and by the peasants as an outer shirt. Originally the shirts, or smocks, were simple, undecorated garments but became increasingly more ornate. In England by the eighteenth century we were seeing beautiful examples of hand stitching and embroidery that are now recognised as smocking. Shepherds' smocks were worn until relatively recently as the shepherd's lifestyle in the early part of this century was little changed from that of a hundred years before. He would wear his best smock, lovingly decorated by his wife or mother, to the fairs and gatherings. Naturally this inspired considerable competition among the ladies of the village to see who could produce the most beautiful smock. Later on, the smocks became available to buy in the towns but were still highly prized garments, costing a great deal of money and were often passed down from father to son.

Holland or linen drill was the fabric used for smocks at this time. As the name implies, this fabric was imported from the Netherlands. Later a heavy cotton fabric, milled in England, gradually replaced it. The smocking and embroidery, even on the commercially-produced smocks, was often done by individual women working in their own homes – an early cottage industry as well as a craft.

The most popular smock was the round smock which was worn 'all the way round', the front being turned around to the back when it was dirty. When that too was dirty, the smock was washed. A very practical idea! Traditionally, the round smock was smocked in panels on the collar, cuffs and yokes. The embroidery often reflected the trade of the wearer or the area of its origin.

Later, with the advent of the industrial revolution, loose clothing, and the lifestyle it embodied, became less and less acceptable. However, children continued to wear smocks particularly to protect their clothes. Small children and babies wore 'dresses' in fine linen smocked around the neck, yoke and cuffs, and these are still worn today.

Smocking is the only form of embroidery that affects the actual shape of a garment, as the drawing in of the fabric fullness needed for smocking will naturally shape it. Today, smocking is being stitched on nightgowns, babies' and children's clothing and even craft projects, and its fascination for the embroiderer continues. Smocking can be as simple or ornate as you like. Two of the simple dresses in this section are from Simplicity Patterns. We have included these as good examples of practical smocking and have altered them slightly. These changes are clearly explained in our instructions.

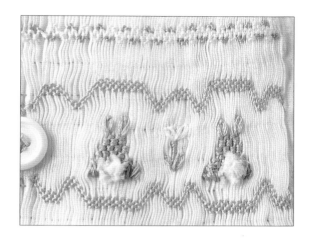

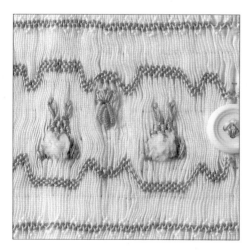

Here are some examples of very intricate and clever smocking. The basic techniques are no different from the simplest smocking, the difference lies in the way in which the smocking has been embroidered with the delightful motifs. Note the clever use of buttons and frayed thread to give added texture and highlights.

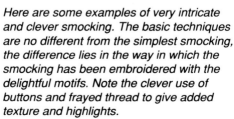

Beautiful Blooms

Embroiderers everywhere are fascinated with flowers and floral shapes. Flowers are the single most frequently recurring motif in embroidery designs. But it's only natural that, as embroiderers love beauty in all forms, they will want to reflect nature's beauty in their stitches. Pretty cushion projects will show you how to bring beautiful blooms indoors with some delightfully simple stitching.

RE-EMBROIDERED CHINTZ CUSHION

This cushion is shaped to suit the motif. We have used fabrics and colours to trim the ruffle that complements the chintz. Make your cushion in the one fabric, big or small, or with a simple contrasting piping if you prefer. Whichever method you choose you are sure to have some very original floral embroideries.

STITCHES USED

Chain Stitch for the stem and vein lines; Long and Short stitch for the petals and leaves

STITCHES

The design of your fabric will suggest the best stitches to use in embroidering. Generally, the stems and fine vein lines are best worked in tiny Chain stitches – either in lines, or in curled 'snail shell' circles to fill in the larger areas. Work petals and other broad areas of colour in Long and Short stitch. This gives you the opportunity to subtly vary the tones of colour, by shading them across the area. French knots are ideal for small dots, or even for filling in the centre of a flower, as the texture from grouped French knots is very attractive. Stem stitch, Back stitch and Satin stitch are also worth considering, and simple Blanket stitch is effective for outlining a flower.

All these stitches are outlined in the Stitch Guide at the front of the book. Work with an embroidery hoop to make your stitching easier and to prevent distortion of the fabric. Try to match closely the colour of the embroidery thread to the colour of your motif – the purpose of this type of embroidery is to embellish and add texture to the design, not to draw attention to any particular stitch.

MATERIALS

sufficient chintz fabric for the cushion front, border, cushion back and frill
sufficient contrasting fabric for the frill
sufficient 2.5 cm wide toning bias binding to go around the embroidered panel
stranded embroidery cotton in the colours of your choice
matching sewing thread
zipper
a cushion insert (purchased cushion insert or one made to measure)

METHOD

Make your cushion any size and shape that complements your fabric. Remember, your embroidered panel will be about 9 cm smaller than the finished cushion.

1 Re-embroider the centre panel of your cushion in the stitches described above. When the embroidery is complete, turn under the outside edges of the panel and press.

2 Press open sufficient 2.5 cm wide toning bias binding. Fold it over double lengthways with right sides together. Press. Pin this bias binding under the edge of the embroidered panel so that the folded edge just protrudes. Overlap the two raw ends and then tuck them neatly out of sight under the embroidered panel. Baste.

3 Cut a piece of fabric the same shape as the embroidered panel but about 10 cm larger all around.

Place the embroidered panel onto the centre of the larger piece, taking care that the border is the same size all around. Stitch through all thicknesses around the embroidered panel.

4 Measure around the edge of the cushion front and cut two and a half times this amount of 10 cm wide fabric for the frill. Cut another identical length 12 cm wide from a contrasting fabric. Join these two strips together along one long edge with right sides facing. Join the short ends, with right sides together, to form a continuous circle. Fold the circular strip over double with wrong sides together so that the raw edges are even and press. You should have a band of contrasting fabric at the outer edge of your frill strip. If your cushion is square, mark the frill strip into quarters. Gather up the frill, starting and stopping your gathering thread at the quarter points. Pin the frill to the right side of the cushion front, placing the quarter points to the corners of the cushion front and having the raw edges even. Adjust the gathers to fit. If your cushion is oblong, mark half-way points along the long sides of the cushion front and mark the frill into two parts. Gather the frill, starting and stopping your gathering thread at the halfway points. Pin the frill around the right side of the cushion front, matching these two points and having the raw edges even. Adjust the gathers to fit.

5 Cut two back pieces, each one the same length as the front but half the width plus 3 cm. Join these pieces in a 3 cm seam, leaving an opening in the centre for the zipper. Insert zipper and leave it open.

6 Fold the frill towards the centre of the embroidered panel. Place the cushion back over the frilled front

panel with right sides facing and raw edges matching. Stitch around the outside edge, following the stitching line for the frill and taking care not to catch the frill as you sew. Turn the cushion to the right side through the zipper opening.

If a commercial cushion insert is not available in a size to suit your cushion, make a calico bag the size of your cushion leaving an opening to insert polyester fibre stuffing or feathers. Once the cushion insert is filled, handsew the opening closed.

THE SECRETS OF CHINTZ

Pretty flowered chintz, so evocative of charming country cottages and summer gardens, is widely regarded as being traditionally and thoroughly English. But chintz has a secret. It is true that chintz is traditional in England, but it is also traditional in Holland where it is called *sits* and in France where it is sometimes referred to as *indiennes* and that is where the secret lies. Yes, chintz originally came from India. The word 'chintz' is a corruption of a Hindi word *chint* or *chinta* meaning 'variegated' or 'spotted all over'. The chints, as they were originally called, were taken to Europe in the 1600s by the various East India companies, English, Dutch and French traders. They were a secondary import as the companies had gone to the East primarily to buy spices but found that Indian textiles, mainly cottons of all types, were part of the deal.

In England, the chints were tried only tentatively on the market, but soon took on and ultimately became the rage. For the first time people had lightweight cotton cloth that could be easily washed. Not only were the pretty patterns attractive but were printed in dyes that were fast. This was a miracle at the time. Europe had never known fast dyes before. Indian dyers had known how to dye cotton fast since ancient times and could produce more than one hundred colours and shades by their age-old methods. Another advantage was that the prices were low, so a large section of the population could afford them. The demand grew and by the mid-1600s the English company had imported well over a quarter of a million pieces. Everybody wanted chints!

There was the same craze in Holland where chintz was being used for clothing; and in France where *indiennes* or *toilet peintes* became the rage for fashionable clothing and for furnishing. The best Indian chintz was painted and resist dyed by a slow and tedious process called *kalamkari* (literally 'penwork'); but to speed up the output to meet the huge European demand block-printing, another old Indian method, was also used. Much admired among the painted clothes were the one-off palampores (from *papangposh* meaning literally 'bedcover'). Many of these featured the 'Tree of Life' design, exotically embellished with luscious fruit, strange birds and animals in glowing colours. These became collectors' items and embroiderers loved to copy them. Embroidery was very popular in England at that time, with bedhangings and covers done in silks or in crewel wool work in flowing designs of English flowers and twining branches. Indian chintz, not dissimilar in design, was now being used.

Indian chintz and other cottons of all types continued to go to Europe for nearly two hundred years until Lancashire mastered cotton spinning and weaving. European textile printers, having found out the secrets of Indian cotton dyeing, were able to produce good copies of Indian chintz. Design differences began to develop in various countries, with English and French chintzes, for instance, gradually evolving into distinctive styles.

Chintz also travelled to faraway colonies such as Australia where large quantities of Indian cottons of all types, including chintz were imported.

In modern chintzes, Indian design influences can still be seen – watch out for stylised flowers, birds and paisley shapes that all reflect their Indian heritage.

Joyce Burnard is a journalist. She founded Ascraft fabrics, a firm which has specialised in importing Indian hand-loomed cotton into Australia. She has just completed a book which traces the fascinating connection of chintz and other Indian textiles with the West.

The chintzes on the opposite page were provided by Ascraft Fabric, Sydney

SILK FLORAL BOUDOIR CUSHION

This charming small cushion can be made from a remnant of lovely silk. Covered with small sprays of flowers, it is embroidered in simple, tiny stitches. Our cushion measures 25 cm x 25 cm but you could expand this size and simply repeat the embroidery motifs to fill the larger area. The lace is stitched on by hand.

STITCHES USED
Bullion stitch for the roses; Lazy Daisy stitch for the daisies; Satin stitch for petals and leaves; French Knots for the dots; Stem stitch for the stems

MATERIALS
two pieces of silk for the back and front
   of the cushion
silk embroidery threads in the colours
   of your choice
sufficient 6 cm wide lace
matching sewing thread
cushion insert to fit
a suitable embroidery needle

METHOD
See the Pull Out Transfer Sheet at the back of the book for the embroidery designs.

1 *For the embroidery:* Transfer the floral motifs onto one piece of silk, following the instructions on the Transfer Sheet. Embroider the flowers in the stitches indicated, following the Stitch Guide at the front of the book.

2 *For the sewing:* When you have finished embroidering, place the cushion front and back together with right sides facing and raw edges even. Stitch around the edge, leaving an opening for turning. Turn cushion right side out. Place the cushion insert inside and close the opening by hand.

3 *To finish off:* Sew the lace around the cushion by aligning the straight edge of the lace with the cushion seam and taking small stitches every 6 mm along the cushion edge, pushing the lace into folds between the stitches. Overlap and neaten the ends of the lace when the stitching is complete.

CROSS STITCH CUSHION

To make this pretty cushion match the colours of your embroidery to a favourite fine cotton print – perhaps to an existing fabric in your home. There is wonderful scope here for a truly unique approach to embroidery.

MATERIALS

36 cm square of white hardanger
  fabric with 22 threads to 2.5 cm
stranded embroidery thread in your
  chosen colours. We used the DMC
  colours as indicated on the graph
2.1 m medium piping cord
2.1 m toning 2.5 cm wide bias binding
2.2 m of 90 cm wide fine cotton
50 cm cushion pad or insert
matching sewing thread
40 cm zipper
a suitable embroidery needle

METHOD

1 *For cutting out:* Cut four strips of fabric each 12 cm x 50 cm for the cushion border. Cut 5 m of 20 cm wide fabric for the frill. Join pieces if necessary to achieve the desired length and two pieces 50 cm x 28 cm for the cushion back.

2 *For the embroidery:* Working with an embroidery hoop, embroider the hardanger panel following the graph and stitch key. On each side, draw out three threads 6 cm from the edge and Hem stitch along the row of holes, following the Stitch Guide at the front of the book.

3 *For the border:* Cut the ends of the border strips in perfect diagonals and join them into an open square, stopping the stitching 1 cm from the inner edge of each corner. Press under 1 cm on the inner edge of the border. Pin and baste this border evenly around the edge of the embroidered panel. Stitch along the pressed edge through all thicknesses.

4 *For the piping:* Open out the bias binding and press it flat. Fold it over double, lengthways. Insert piping cord into the fold and stitch it in place, using the zipper foot of your sewing machine. Baste this piping around the edge of the right side of the cushion front, clipping into the corners for ease.

5 *For the frill:* Join the frill strips into one continuous circle. Press it over double with wrong sides together and raw edges even. Divide and mark the circle into quarters with pins. Gather around the circle, starting and finishing at the quarter points. Pin the frill to right side corners of the cushion front, matching quarter points and with raw edges even. Adjust the

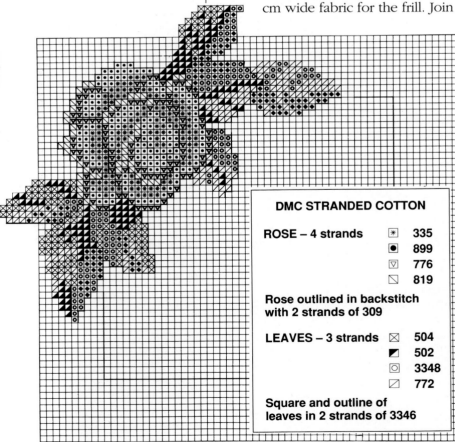

DMC STRANDED COTTON

ROSE – 4 strands ✳ 335
  ⬤ 899
  ▽ 776
  ◺ 819

Rose outlined in backstitch with 2 strands of 309

LEAVES – 3 strands ⊠ 504
  ◣ 502
  ⊙ 3348
  ◿ 772

Square and outline of leaves in 2 strands of 3346

gathers to fit. Stitch the frill in place, taking care not to stitch through the piping cord.

6 *For the cushion back:* Stitch the back sections together along the 50 cm edge, using a 3 cm seam allowance, and leaving a 40 cm gap for the zipper at the centre of the seam. Press the seam open and insert the zipper.

Leave the zipper open.

7 *To assemble the cushion:* Fold the frill towards the centre of the embroidered panel. Place back and front together with right sides facing and raw edges even. Stitch around the edge following the previous stitching. Turn the cushion right side out through the zipper opening.

Embroider a Stencil

Hand appliqué has always looked exquisite because it is so detailed and intricate. This can be an obstacle, preventing beginners taking up this pleasing embroidery. Here is the answer! This lovely cloth has been stencilled and re-embroidered to give the same textured effect.

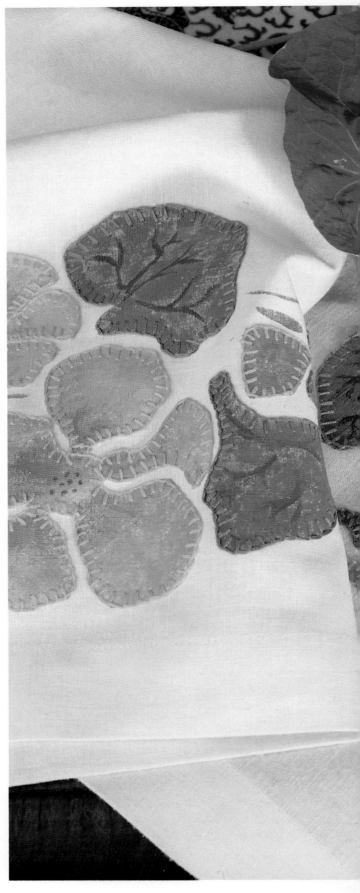

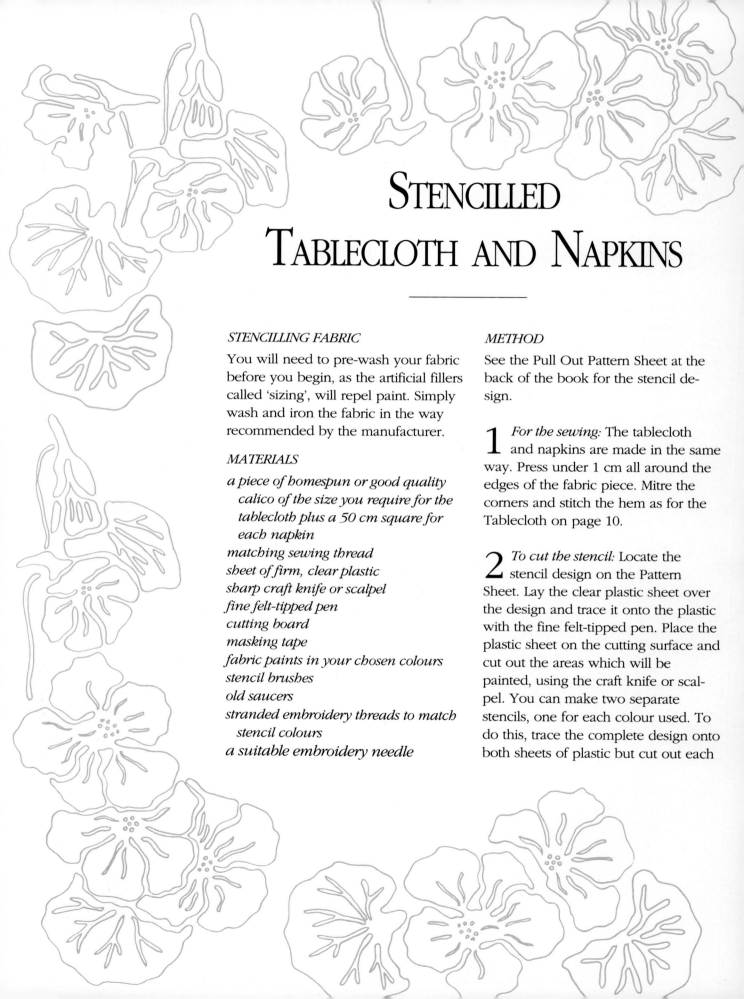

STENCILLED
TABLECLOTH AND NAPKINS

STENCILLING FABRIC

You will need to pre-wash your fabric before you begin, as the artificial fillers called 'sizing', will repel paint. Simply wash and iron the fabric in the way recommended by the manufacturer.

MATERIALS

a piece of homespun or good quality calico of the size you require for the tablecloth plus a 50 cm square for each napkin
matching sewing thread
sheet of firm, clear plastic
sharp craft knife or scalpel
fine felt-tipped pen
cutting board
masking tape
fabric paints in your chosen colours
stencil brushes
old saucers
stranded embroidery threads to match stencil colours
a suitable embroidery needle

METHOD

See the Pull Out Pattern Sheet at the back of the book for the stencil design.

1 *For the sewing:* The tablecloth and napkins are made in the same way. Press under 1 cm all around the edges of the fabric piece. Mitre the corners and stitch the hem as for the Tablecloth on page 10.

2 *To cut the stencil:* Locate the stencil design on the Pattern Sheet. Lay the clear plastic sheet over the design and trace it onto the plastic with the fine felt-tipped pen. Place the plastic sheet on the cutting surface and cut out the areas which will be painted, using the craft knife or scalpel. You can make two separate stencils, one for each colour used. To do this, trace the complete design onto both sheets of plastic but cut out each

one for a single colour only. The rest of the traced design will help you position the stencil.

3 *For painting the stencil:* Position the motifs in the corners of your fabric. Note that the napkins are stencilled in one corner only and the border goes around all four sides. Hold the stencil in place with small strips of masking tape. If you are using a single stencil for both colours, it is helpful to cover adjoining areas of the other colour with masking tape. Pour a small quantity of paint into a saucer and spread it out. Stencils require very little paint compared to other painting techniques. Using a dry brush and a dabbing, rather than a stroking, move-ment paint in the design, working from the edges towards the centre of an area. Wipe off any excess paint. Too much paint on the brush or even a wet brush will cause the paint to seep under the edges of the stencil and give an indistinct outline. Allow the paint to dry between colours to avoid running. Additional highlights can be painted over the top of the stencilled design to give depth and texture to the shapes, for example we painted over yellow with a deeper orange. Keep your stencil clean –

wash it between uses, especially if you are using one stencil for both colours.

4 *To stencil the border:* Work out your colour and pattern distribu-tion before you begin painting. Stencil all around first with one colour, allow it to dry then replace the stencil in the spaces you have left and fill in the second colour. Try moving the stencil for different angles of flowers and leaves, and taking elements out of the design and repositioning them. The stencilled border should link up with the bunch of flowers on both sides.

5 *For the embroidery:* Stitch around the leaves and flowers using blanket stitch as shown in the Stitch Guide at the front of the book. Choose colours to match the colours of the paints. Remember you want this stitching to be visible so don't make the individual stitches too small. Be sure to follow the edges of the flowers and leaves accurately.

Charming Cross Stitch

Of all the embroidery stitches, Cross stitch is the most popular. Use it on a sampler, a tapestry or a delicately embroidered linen handkerchief and matching jewellery cushion.

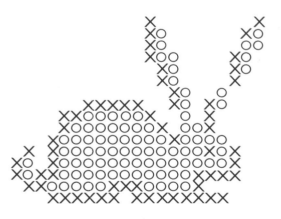

MONOGRAMMED HANDKERCHIEF

The perfect gifts to embroider for someone special, this dainty handkerchief and jewellery cushion are sure to be treasured for a long time. You can make your own handkerchief or buy one to embroider.

MATERIALS

a square of handkerchief linen
wide single edged lace to trim the edge
10 cm square of waste canvas
stranded embroidery thread in the
*   colours of your choice*
a suitable embroidery needle

METHOD

See the Pull Out Pattern Sheet at the back of the book for the Cross stitch alphabet graph.

1 *For the lace:* Draw threads from each edge of the linen square and re-trim to make certain all the edges are perfectly straight. Press in 5 mm all around the square. Stitch the lace under the pressed edge, pleating or gathering it at the corners.

2 *For the embroidery:* Baste the edges of a piece of waste canvas, large enough to accommodate your letter, over one corner of the handkerchief. Locate the letter you require on the Pattern Sheet and embroider it over the waste canvas, through the linen as well, using three strands of embroidery thread. When the embroidery is complete, carefully draw out the canvas, thread by thread, leaving the Cross stitch motif on the linen.

JEWELLERY CUSHION

MATERIALS

two pieces of linen each 13 cm x
*   10 cm*
two strips of linen each 10 cm x 5 cm
two strips of linen each 13 cm x 5 cm
10 cm square of waste canvas
stranded embroidery thread in the
*   colours of your choice*
1.3 m coloured twisted cord
small quantity of polyester fibre for
*   stuffing*
iron on interfacing
matching sewing thread
a suitable embroidery needle

METHOD

See the Pull Out Pattern Sheet at the back of the book for the Cross stitch alphabet graph.
1 cm seams allowed all around each pattern piece.

1 *For the embroidery:* Find the centre of one square of linen by folding it in half lengthways and widthways. The intersection of the folds is the centre point. Baste the edges of a piece of waste canvas, large enough to accommodate your letter, over this centre point. Locate the letter you require on the Pattern Sheet and embroider it over the waste canvas, through the linen as well, using three strands of embroidery thread. When the embroidery is complete, carefully draw out the canvas thread by thread, leaving the Cross stitch motif on the linen.

2 *For the sewing:* Interface all pieces of linen. Pin the short ends of all the strips together to form an open box. Check that it fits around the edge of the embroidered linen. Adjust the

STITCHES USED
Cross stitch for all motifs

Above: Jewellery Cushion
Right: Monogrammed Handkerchief

length if necessary. Pin the strip around the edge of the embroidered linen, with raw edges even, right sides facing and seams matching to the corners. Stitch in a 1 cm seam. Pin the remaining piece of linen to the remaining edge of the strip with right sides together, raw edges even and seams matching to the corners again. Stitch, leaving an opening for turning. Turn the cushion to the right side, pushing the corners out neatly. Stuff the cushion firmly and close the opening by hand. Hand sew the twisted cord around the top edge of the cushion, taking it into three small loops at each corner, resembling a clover leaf. Start and finish at a corner, tucking the ends of the cord out of sight behind a loop at the end.

THE STORY OF SAMPLERS

Samplers were, just as their name implies, a piece of fabric stitched to demonstrate various sewing techniques that allowed the stitchers to display their talents. For a long time, samplers actually functioned as job applications, being presented to a prospective employer to show off the talents of the seamstress. Up until quite recently, girls who were schooled in the traditional sewing crafts would make a darning sampler, a Cross stitch sampler and perhaps a fancy embroidery sampler.

Often samplers were totally spontaneous, with the design taking shape as the stitcher worked her way through the project. These samplers could show simple rows of stitches, tucks, gathers, collections of a particular motif – perhaps animals, flowers or houses, or they could even depict the family tree, dates of birth and the occupations and interests of the family members.

If these talented women were sentimental enough to keep their works of art, chances are they are beautifully framed and displayed in their homes as a permanent reminder of their skills.

Samplers still have the element of variety, but perhaps not so much as yesterday. Today they show names and dates, wise sayings, alphabets or special motifs to commemorate a great occasion. Samplers still demand the same skills and, of course, the more accurate the work the better the finished product looks. Cross stitch has become the modern day sampler stitch, with endless examples available in kits, or as counted Cross stitch in embroidery books. It's important to have your sampler properly framed and preserved. Cast your eye over our photographs of samplers past and present, and perhaps you'll be inspired to embark on your own sentimental journey.

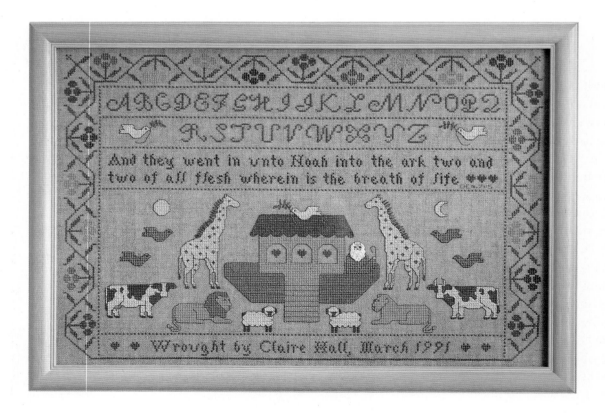

Samplers from Simply Stitches

On this page and on the opposite page are some delightful examples of embroidered samplers, showing the almost limitless variety that you can achieve with simple Cross stitch. You can choose something as simple as the alphabet (below) or one as intricate as the Bird in Hand sampler at the bottom of the page. Ideally, the motifs should reflect some aspect of your life and interests or contain some message that you wish to convey. In the past, these messages were often religious ones, such as the Lord's prayer or the story of Noah's ark (opposite page).

FESTIVE SAMPLER

This charming mix of a monogram and a floral spray gives a fresh, contemporary feel to an otherwise traditional sampler motif. Alternatively, you can take letters from the alphabet and spell out the name of someone special, keeping the floral border and sprays. This would give the sampler a horizontal shape, rather than the vertical shape it is now .

STITCHES USED
Cross stitch for all the motifs

MATERIALS
a piece of DMC Lugana 40 cm x 50 cm
DMC stranded embroidery cotton in the following colours: 3350; 963; 899; 761; 3364; 3362; 472; 800; 793
a suitable embroidery needle

METHOD
See the Pull Out Pattern Sheet at the back of the book for the Cross stitch alphabet graph.

1 *To find the centre:* Mark the centre of your fabric vertically and horizontally with a line of basting. Where these lines intersect is the middle of your fabric. Draw a pencil line connecting the arrows on each side of the graph. This point is the centre of the graph and should correspond with the centre of the fabric. Start counting from this point.

2 *For the embroidery:* Each square on the graph contains a symbol that denotes a colour to be worked in Cross stitch. Embroider, using three strands of thread and Cross stitch, following the Stitch Guide at the front of the book. Do not tie knots but begin and end a thread by running the needle through the back of a few stitches at the back of the work. Using a tapestry roller frame or a large embroidery hoop will make the work easier.

3 *For the framing:* On completion of the embroidery, it is important to have your sampler framed by someone specialising in this type of work.

This Festive Cross Stitch Sampler is from DMC Needle-craft Pty Ltd and is worked in DMC threads.

CORNELLI
WOOL EMBROIDERY

This is a very simple yet effective trim for any woollen garment – and it can be used on lighter fabrics too. Cornelli work is the effect of one long continuous line of stitching, forming a pattern of loops and curves.

STITCHES USED
Chain stitch

MATERIALS
a purchased woollen jumper or
    cardigan
suitable yarn for working the stitches
tapestry needle

METHOD

1 *For the design:* Mark out your pattern area with basting. If you are not confident enough to make the design as you go, mark out your cornelli lines with a soft lead pencil or chalk. You will find it becomes much easier with a little practice. The design given here is a guide – adjust it to suit your pattern area.

2 *For the embroidery:* The basic stitch used in the embroidery is Chain stitch, though any 'straight' stitch can be effective. We chose Chain stitch as it is fairly bulky and results come quickly. Two different weights of yarn were used – one a textured chenille knitting yarn and another knitting yarn made from smooth glossy silk. Stitch two parallel lines in a random wavy line that keeps turning back on itself until the basted area is covered.

3 *To finish off:* Consider changing the buttons on your cardigan to complement the embroidery. Make the shape of your embroidery suit your garment. For a small area such as a shoulder or the point at centre front, bring the stitching into a point where you can later attach a tassel made from yarn to complete the effect!

Left: See how Cornelli work is simply the effect of two wiggly lines of Chain stitch working together to form the pattern

63

Here are some additional embroidery designs for you to use. You can embroider them using many of the stitches found in the Stitch Guide at the front of the book.

ACKNOWLEDGMENTS

The publishers would like to thank the following people who assisted with production of this book: David Jones own brand for the woollen jumpers; Liberty for the fabric for the smocked dresses; DMC for embroidery supplies; Offray for ribbons; Simplicity Patterns Australia for the dress patterns; Antiques loaned by Robyn Macintosh, Michelle Gleason and Barbara Shorter.

HOW TO USE THE TRANSFER SHEET

- Preheat iron. Set to recommended temperature for each fabric.

- Do not use steam.

- Cut out chosen design and position it on to fabric, INK SIDE DOWN.

- Place the iron directly on the transfer pattern – press, lift and look (check how dark the design looks by carefully lifting one corner while holding the rest of the design in place). Do not slide the iron the same way you do when you are ironing! THE DESIGN COULD SMEAR.

- After the entire design is transferred, let it cool a little before removing the pattern.

- Transfers can be used more than once, but they get lighter each time. To extend the life, iron-on transfer pencils are available at fabric and craft stores. Simply trace over pattern lines with special pencil and transfer.

- The lines on the transfers will fade with each use. Since we have used the transfer lines as details in some of our designs, we suggest the use of a permanent fabric outline pen to fill them in or darken them. These pens are available at craft and fabric stores.